Stamps

Mir Tamim Ansary

RIGBY
INTERACTIVE
LIBRARY

© 1997 Rigby Education
Published by Rigby Interactive Library,
an imprint of Rigby Education,
division of Reed Elsevier, Inc.
500 Coventry Lane
Crystal Lake, IL 60014

Art director for the series: Rhea Banker

Contributing designers: Susan Darwin Ordahl, Barbara Rusin, Chuck Yuen

Book designer: Barbara Rusin

The text for this book is set in Garamond Book.

Printed in Hong Kong

00 99 98 97 96
10 9 8 7 6 5 4 3 2 1

Library of Congress Cataloging-in-Publication Data
Ansary, Mir Tamim
    Stamps / Mir Tamim Ansary.
      p.   cm. -- (Cool collections.)
    Includes bibliographical references and index.
    Summary: Presents tips for collecting, organizing, and displaying
postage stamps.
    ISBN 1-57572-113-9
    1. Stamp collecting--Juvenile literature.   [1. Stamp collecting.]
I. Title. II. Series: Ansary, Mir Tamim. Cool collections.
HE6215.A57   1997
769.56--dc21   96-39410
                                                   CIP
                                                    AC

Acknowledgments
The publisher would like to thank the following for permission to reproduce photographs of
their stamp collections: Rhea Banker, John Caminiti, Weston S. Evans, Ines Greenberger, Jack
Intrator and Judy Rosenbaum.

Cover and all interior photographs: Stephen Ogilvy

Note to the Reader
Some words in this book are printed in **bold** type. This indicates that the word is listed in the
glossary on page 24. The glossary gives a brief explanation of words that may be new to you
and tells you the page on which each word first appears.

Visit Rigby's Education Station ® on the World Wide Web at http://www.rigby.com

Contents

Starting a Stamp Collection

This is a postage stamp.

Stamps are required in order to send mail, but they're fun to look at, too.

That's why millions of people are stamp **collectors**. Starting your own stamp collection is easy. Just talk to people who get letters. Ask them to give the stamps to you.

5

Selecting Stamps

The hard part about starting a stamp collection is making choices. There are so many different kinds of stamps.

What kinds of stamps will interest you? What kind of collection will you build?

Collector's Tip

Here are four things you may need as a stamp collector:

- Stamp **tongs**
- **Glassine** envelopes
- Stamp albums
- **Magnifying glass**

Stamps from Around

You can look for stamps from other countries. This is called *collecting the world*. Could you get one from every country?

Venezuela

Belgium

Denmark

Mongolia

Republic of Congo

Romania

Monaco

France

Canada

Republic of Chad

Spain

the World

You may need to narrow your search. For example, you could focus on collecting holiday stamps. Your collection could show holidays around the world.

New Guinea

Greece

Romania

Israel

Rwanda

Collector's Tip

To get a stamp off an envelope, drop it in warm water. The stamp side should be down. The stamp will come off and sink. Then put it between two paper towels. Set a book on top so it will dry flat. Leave it there overnight.

Republic of Congo

Stamps from One Place

You can collect the stamps of just one country. Here are stamps from the United Kingdom. What country's stamps would you collect?

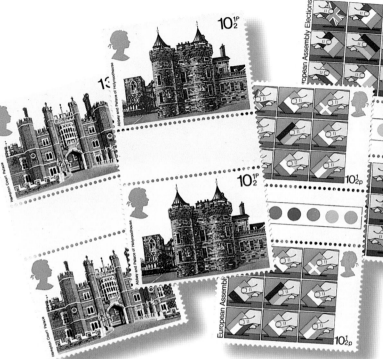

Or you could look for stamps that show beautiful places. Make a collection of places you would like to visit someday.

Collector's Tip

Here's an idea. Find a pen pal in another country. As you trade letters, you will also trade stamps. Ask your pen pal to use different kinds of stamps on every letter.

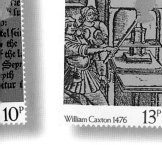

Stamps from the

Here are common stamps of the United States. You can buy them at the post office.

United States

Here are common U.S. stamps of the past. These stamps are no longer made. But you can still get them from other collectors.

Collector's Tip

Stamps etc. is a catalog. It shows all the U.S. postage stamps you can buy today. Your local post office can tell you how to get this catalog.

Commemorative Stamps

These stamps honor a special person or event.
Stamps like these are called *commemoratives*.
They are made only once, for about a year. Get
them when they're new.

Some people collect *covers*, or whole envelopes. They like to see who wrote to whom and where the letter went. They like to guess what the letter said.

Collector's Tip

There are many ways to get old commemorative stamps. Rummage in attics. Check old boxes and trunks. Go to garage sales. Or buy a bag of used stamps from a stamp store. This is called a *mixture*. Looking through one of these is like hunting for treasure.

Special-Interest Stamps

You may wish to collect stamps about a favorite topic. Are you interested in dinosaurs? Flowers? Birds?

Are you interested in sports? Space travel? Ships? You're in luck. Your collection will be huge!

Collector's Tip

Some **canceled** stamps are worth more than others. A good one is clean, flat, and untorn. The mark that canceled it is light. The lines are thin, not smudged. The picture is not spoiled or covered.

Historical Stamps

Do you wonder about things that happened long ago? Some stamps show events from history. You can tell the story of the world with a stamp collection.

FIRST KENTUCKY SETTLEMENT FORT HARROD 1774 1974

US 10c

Is it too hard to *collect the world*? Then try telling the story of just one country. These stamps show events from U.S. history.

Gallery of

Many stamps show famous people. You can make a stamp Hall of Fame. Which of these people have you heard about? Do you know why they're famous?

LOUIS ARMSTRONG

John Steinbeck

32 USA

JELLY ROLL MORTON

JAZZ COMPOSER AND PIANIST

32

JAZZ COMPOSER AND PIANIST

EUB BLAK

32

Sitting Bull

USA 28

Einstein

Martin Luther King Jr.

AMES DEAN

LONIOUS MON

Red Cloud

10 USA

ELEANOR ROOSEVELT

5¢

Faces and Paintings

Great works of art appear on stamps, too. Collect them and you can make a tiny gallery. You might someday see the paintings or statues in real life.

Collector's Tip

Stamp shows bring collectors together. They come to trade, sell, and chat about stamps. A stamp store clerk can tell you about shows coming up in your area.

Displaying Your Stamps

You can buy a stamp album that has pictures of
stamps. Filling an album of this kind is like a game.
You look for a stamp to match each picture.

You can also buy a blank album. Then you can group your stamps any way you want. The finished album will be one of a kind—just like you!

 Collector's Tip

Some stamps seem to look alike. But they actually have tiny differences. Use a magnifying glass to check the details.

Glossary

Canceled Made unusable. Stamps that have been sent through the mail are canceled so they cannot be used again. 17

Collectors People who collect a certain type of object. Collectors sort, study, and **display** their collections. 5

Display To show off an object in a clear and interesting way. 22

Glassine Thin, see-through paper that air and grease can't get through. Glassine envelopes protect stamps in a collection. 7

Hinges Device on which a swinging lid turns. 19

Magnifying glass Special tool used to see the details of an object. 7

Tongs Tools made up of two pieces joined with a hinge. Tongs are used to hold objects, such as stamps and beads. 7

Index

More Books to Read

Benarti, Carol. *World Stamps.* New York: Random House, 1994.

Jacobsen, Karen. *Stamps.* Chicago: Childrens Press, 1983.

Poskanzer, Susan. *Superduper Collectors.* Mahwah, N.J.: Troll, 1986.